ANIMAL HABITATS

# PENGUINS
## AND THEIR HOMES

Deborah Chase Gibson

The Rosen Publishing Group's
**PowerKids Press**™
New York

Published in 1999 by The Rosen Publishing Group, Inc.
29 East 21st Street, New York, NY 10010

First Edition

Book Design: Kim Sonsky

Photo Credits:  Cover and title page © Animals Animals/D. Allan;  p. 4 © Animals Animals/Eastcott/Momatiuk; p. 5 © Animals Animals/Zig Leszczynski; pp. 6, 9 © FPG/Telegraph Colour Library; p. 8 © Animals Animals/John Gerlach; p. 10 © Animals Animals/Arthur Holzman; pp. 13, 14 © Animals Animals/G.L. Kooyman; pp. 16, 18, 21 © Animals Animals/Johnny Johnson; p. 22 © FPG/Richard Harrington; p. 24 © FPG/Stan Osolinski.

Gibson, Deborah Chase.
     Penguins and their homes / Deborah Chase Gibson.
          p. cm. — (Animal habitats)
     Includes index.
     Summary: Presents an overview of different kinds of penguins and how and where they make their homes.
     ISBN 0-8239-5311-4
     1. Penguins—Juvenile literature. 2. Penguins—Habitat—Juvenile literature. [1. Penguins.] I. Title. II. Series: Gibson, Deborah Chase. Animal habitats.
     QL696.S473G46  1998
     598.47—dc21                                                          98-15387
                                                                              CIP
                                                                              AC

Manufactured in the United States of America

# CONTENTS

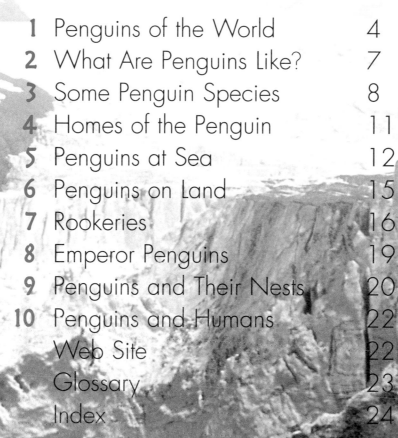

| 1  | Penguins of the World      | 4  |
|----|----------------------------|----|
| 2  | What Are Penguins Like?    | 7  |
| 3  | Some Penguin Species       | 8  |
| 4  | Homes of the Penguin       | 11 |
| 5  | Penguins at Sea            | 12 |
| 6  | Penguins on Land           | 15 |
| 7  | Rookeries                  | 16 |
| 8  | Emperor Penguins           | 19 |
| 9  | Penguins and Their Nests   | 20 |
| 10 | Penguins and Humans        | 22 |
|    | Web Site                   | 22 |
|    | Glossary                   | 23 |
|    | Index                      | 24 |

# PENGUINS OF THE WORLD

When you think of a penguin, you may picture the black-and-white emperor penguin waddling along the icy **tundra** (TUN-druh) of the South Pole. It is true that penguin **habitats** (HA-bih-tats) are found only in the southern half of the world. However, they don't live only on the **continent** (KON-tih-nent) of Antarctica. There are actually 17 different **species** (SPEE-sheez), or kinds, of penguins.

The little penguin's habitat is southern Australia and New

Little penguins weigh just over two pounds.

4

Zealand. Another species, the Galapagos penguin, lives near the **equator** (ih-KWAY-ter), in the hottest part of the world.

The black-footed African penguin lives in South Africa. ▶

At three feet tall, king penguins
are one of the largest penguins. ▶

# WHAT ARE PENGUINS LIKE?

Even though penguins are birds, they cannot fly through the air. Penguins swim to get around.

Penguins are usually black on their backs and white on their fronts. This coloring helps them hide from their enemies while they swim in the ocean. But black and white aren't the only colors found on penguins. The king penguin has orange patches on either side of its head that look like the colors in a sunset. The top of its chest is yellow and orange. The little penguin of Australia and New Zealand has a bluish back. That's why the little penguin is sometimes called the blue penguin.

# SOME PENGUIN SPECIES

Penguins have thousands of tiny feathers that keep them warm. Penguins living in colder habitats have feathers on their beaks and feet too. The largest penguin in the world is the emperor penguin of Antarctica. This penguin stands four feet tall. The little penguin is the smallest, and he stands about one foot tall.

The feisty rockhopper penguin does just what his name says. Instead of waddling like other penguins, this penguin jumps from rock to rock. The royal penguins of Australia's Macquarie Island have long, yellow eyebrows that stick out like cat whiskers from their foreheads.

Rockhopper penguins weigh about six pounds.

Emperor penguins can weigh as much as 100 pounds. ▼

# HOMES OF THE PENGUIN

Penguins really have two homes: the land and the sea. Their habitats must provide penguins with **access** (AK-sess) to both. They stay on land to **breed** (BREED) and raise baby penguins. Penguins also rest on land or great sheets of ice floating on the ocean. Baby penguins need to be about two or three months old before they can swim deep into the sea.

Penguins spend most of their time in the sea. Penguins hunt and **forage** (FOR-ij) in and around the sea. In fact, all the food penguins eat comes from the sea.

◀ Emperor penguins usually raise their young on or near the ice.

# PENGUINS AT SEA

The shape of penguins' bodies allows them to move easily through the water. Penguins use their feet to steer through the water. Penguins dive and zip around underwater so fast that they leave a trail of air bubbles behind them.

Penguins swim around looking for their favorite underwater foods, such as fish, squid, and tiny sea animals called **krill** (KRIL). But the penguins have to watch out for **predators** (PREH-duh-ters). The penguin's predators include leopard seals, fur seals, killer whales, sea lions, and sharks. These sea animals like to eat penguins.

Penguins, such as the Galapagos penguin, use their stiff wings as powerful paddles.

# PENGUINS ON LAND

Penguins are skilled swimmers. But getting around on land is not as easy for them. Penguins have short legs. Penguins have to take lots of small steps to walk a short distance. That's why they look like they are waddling rather than walking.

Penguins do have very strong feet. Their three toes act like hooks. This lets penguins get a solid grip on rocky or icy land. Penguins can also climb rocks or ice, using their beaks as hooks to steady themselves.

◄ Sometimes penguins, like these emperor penguins, slide along the ice on their bellies. The penguins use their feet and flippers to push.

# ROOKERIES

Some penguins, such as the emperor and Adelie penguins, use land for their breeding sites, called **rookeries** (ROOK-er-eez). Rookeries are usually miles from the ocean, on the ice. Since there aren't any trees, a rookery is usually made under an ice cliff. Six thousand penguins can gather in one rookery.

This is an emperor penguin rookery.

Around October, the Adelie penguins of Antarctica begin heading toward rookeries. These penguins can walk for hundreds of miles across the ice. At the rookery, the males build nests, where the females usually lay two eggs. The eggs hatch in about one month. In February, the penguins return to their homes by the sea.

# EMPEROR PENGUINS

Emperor penguins **mate** (MAYT) around March. By May, the female lays an egg. She lays only one egg at a time. For the next 40 to 50 days, the male emperor penguin keeps the egg warm using a fold of skin in his belly. Males don't eat during this time. The female returns before the egg hatches, and stays with the chick when it's born. The hungry male returns to the sea to feed.

◀ Here is an emperor penguin baby, or chick, in Antarctica.

# PENGUINS AND THEIR NESTS

Not all penguins breed and nest out in the open. Some make their nests in **burrows** (BUR-ohs) in the ground. The Magellanic penguins nest in the southern part of South America and islands nearby. These penguins dig burrows in soft ground that are about three to six feet deep. Inside the burrow, the penguins make soft nests of grass. During mating season, they lay their eggs in these nests. The burrows protect Magellanic penguin chicks from the hot sun and predators, such as foxes.

Male Adelie penguins build nests at rookeries. These penguins use their beaks to pick up pebbles and small stones. Then they make mounds for nests. Once the female lays the eggs, the male and female take turns lying on the eggs in the nest to keep them warm.

Rockhopper penguins build their nests on land. ▶

# PENGUINS AND HUMANS

In the past, humans have invaded penguin habitats and killed millions of penguins for their **blubber** (BLUH-ber). This layer of fat keeps penguins warm. People used this blubber as fuel for heat and lamps.

Today there are laws protecting penguins. But penguin habitats aren't always protected. Humans are fishing more often in the same waters where penguins feed. This means there is less food for penguins to eat. Sadly, pollution of the seas near Antarctica has put penguins and their habitats in danger.

Scientists are studying penguins and how they live. If we can protect their habitats, we may be able to keep penguins from becoming an **endangered** (en-DAYN-jerd) species.

## WEB SITE:

You can learn more about penguins at this Web site: www.vni.net/~kwelch/penguins/

# GLOSSARY

**access** (AK-sess)  A way to get to someplace easily.

**blubber** (BLUH-ber)  Penguin fat.

**breed** (BREED)  When a male and female animal have babies.

**burrow** (BUR-oh)  A hole an animal digs in the ground to use as a nesting site.

**continent** (KON-tih-nent)  A very large area of land.

**endangered** (en-DAYN-jerd)  When something is in danger of no longer existing.

**equator** (ih-KWAY-ter)  An imaginary line that separates Earth into two parts: north and south.

**forage** (FOR-ij)  To search for food.

**habitat** (HA-bih-tat)  The surroundings where an animal lives.

**krill** (KRIL)  Tiny sea animals that penguins eat.

**mate** (MAYT)  A special joining of a male and female body. After mating, the female may have a baby grow inside her.

**predator** (PREH-duh-ter)  An animal that kills other animals for food.

**rookery** (ROOK-er-ee)  A place where penguins go to breed and raise their young.

**species** (SPEE-sheez)  A group of animals that are very much alike.

**tundra** (TUN-druh)  The frozen land of the coldest parts of the world.

# INDEX

**A**
access, 11
Adelie penguins, 16–17, 20

**B**
blubber, 22
breed, 11, 16–17, 20
burrow, 20

**C**
continent, 4

**E**
emperor penguin, 4, 8, 16–17
endangered, 22
equator, 5

**F**
forage, 11

**G**
Galapagos penguin, 5

**H**
habitat, 4, 8, 11, 12, 15, 22

**K**
king penguin, 7
krill, 12

**L**
little penguin, 4–5, 7, 8

**M**
Magellanic penguins, 20
mate, 19, 20

**P**
predators, 12, 20

**R**
rockhopper penguin, 8
rookeries, 16-17, 20
royal penguin, 8

**S**
species, 4, 22

**T**
tundra, 4